THE SPIRITUALITY OF ST PATRICK

In memory of Philip Day,
best of company,
most loyal of friends

Lesley Whiteside

The Spirituality of

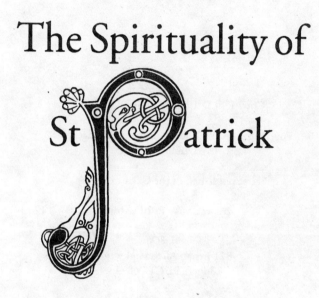

St Patrick

MOREHOUSE PUBLISHING

First published by The Columba Press, Blackrock,
Co. Dublin, Ireland

First published in the U.S. in 1997 by

Morehouse Publishing

Editorial Office
871 Ethan Allen Highway
Ridgefield, CT 06877

Corporate Office
P.O. Box 1321
Harrisburg, PA 17105

A catalog record for this book is available from
the Library of Congress

ISBN: 0-8192-1693-3

Printed in the United States of America

Contents

Introduction

ASK ALMOST anyone about Patrick and you will get a picture of the patron saint of Ireland as a mitred bishop, whose mission took him across Ireland from Mount Slemish in County Antrim to Croagh Patrick in County Mayo, near the Atlantic Ocean. This is the Patrick of the stained glass window, using the shamrock to teach the pagan Irish the doctrine of the Trinity and ridding the country of snakes, but it is not the real Patrick.

In the centuries after his death, so great a cult grew round him that scholars found it difficult to separate historical fact from pious myth. The only certain biographical facts are gleaned from two authenticated works by Patrick himself – his *Confession* and the *Letter to Coroticus*. Even then there are difficulties, because, in the first place, neither document was primarily concerned with his life story, and, in the second place, the earliest manuscript we have dates from the ninth century. By that time, the writings had been copied many times, giving rise to mistakes and omissions.

Patrick's origins

It is probable that one of these mistakes was in transcribing the name of Patrick's birthplace, 'Bannavem Taberniae'. The exact location is unknown, but clearly it was near the west coast of Britain, as it was in the area vulnerable to Irish raids. 'Bannavem Taberniae' doesn't make sense as a Latin placename but, if the reading 'Banna Venta Bernia' is correct, Patrick was born at Birdoswald, near Carlisle, in Cumbria.

An even more intractable question is the date of Patrick's mission to Ireland. Tradition fixes his mission from 432 to 461 and, consequently, his birth at c.390. It has to be remembered that the seventh-century annalists who gave these dates were anxious to fix Patrick's arrival as early as possible after 431, when Pope Celestinus sent Palladius as the first bishop of the Irish Christians. Recent scholarship has inclined to place his mission from c.461 to 493 and, consequently, his birth to c.415. This debate need not distract us from the central point: that Patrick was a fifth-century Irish saint. He was not the first to evangelise the Irish but, in conformity with the practice of the time, was appointed as bishop to a Christian community.

Irrespective of any success that Palladius may have had (nothing further is known about him), Ireland was no longer an entirely pagan country and there were at least some parts, particularly in the southern and eastern coastal areas, in which conversions had been made.

Patrick's boyhood

The fall of the Roman Empire made little difference to life in Britain. By the late fourth century, imperial control in that far outpost of the once great Empire had become so diminished that government was in the hands of local officials (*decuriones*), who were responsible for the maintenance of law and order and the collection of taxes.

Patrick's aristocratic status is attested by the fact that his father, Calpurnius, was one of these officials and the family lived in a villa (a house with its own farm estate), staffed by slaves. Patrick's father was a deacon in the church and his grandfather, Potitus, was a priest. By the beginning of the fifth century, in advance of the Anglo-Saxon invasions, the church in Britain was well established and enjoyed a fair degree of autonomy under the leadership of its bishops.

Patrick's education was probably conducted at home through Latin. He was given a grounding in the Christian faith but admits that he 'did not then know the true God,' (*Conf* 1) and deserved punishment for ignoring his commandments. The punishment, as he saw it, came just short of his sixteenth birthday, when the crew of an Irish ship seized him at his home and carried him off to captivity in Ireland, one of many thousands so enslaved.

A slave in Ireland

Patrick became a slave in a remote part of Ireland. Although he does not tell us where it was, he does recount that, years after his escape, his call to return came when he heard 'the voice of those who were by the Wood of Voclut which is near the Western Sea', calling, 'Holy boy, we are asking you to come and walk among us again.' (*Conf* 23) This clearly implies that the wood, which was perhaps in Mayo, had been the place of his captivity.

It must have been a tough and lonely existence for Patrick, out in all weathers day and night looking after his flock, but it was here that he came to know God and would say 'in one day as many as a hundred prayers and nearly as many at night.' (*Conf* 16) He began to experience visions and dreams, and one night in his sleep he heard a voice saying, 'You will soon return to your own country', and again, 'Your ship is ready.' (*Conf* 17) Led by the Spirit, he made his way to a port, some two hundred miles away, where he saw the ship on the point of sailing. Even then his faith was tested for, when he asked for a passage, the captain shouted 'No way!' (*Conf* 18) Patrick went away and prayed and soon the captain relented.

They sailed for three days until they reached port. Their ultimate destination is unknown: All Patrick tells us is that, after twenty-eight days of travelling through uninhabited country, they ran out of food. The captain, in despair, asked Patrick why his God was allowing them to die of hunger. Patrick replied, 'Turn in faith with all your heart to the Lord my God, that he may today send food across your way,' whereupon a herd of pigs appeared and they were saved from starvation! (*Conf* 19)

Obscure years

While Patrick writes in some detail about this phase
of his life, he tells virtually nothing about subsequent
events until he returned to Ireland. He mentions that
he was again living with his parents, but says nothing
of his training for the ministry nor of his ordination.
It is understandable that the British church proposed
him for an episcopacy among the Irish, as he was so
familiar with the country and must have spoken
Irish.

A bishop to the Irish

The Ireland to which Patrick returned as bishop was
a rural society, Irish in speech and in culture, though
much influenced by Roman society through trade,
licit and illicit. Alongside imports and exports, a
flourishing slave trade had long existed, with Irish
chiefs leading raids on the west coast of Britain. Some
of these slaves must have brought a Christian as well
as a Roman influence.

The country was controlled by a plethora of warrior
kings and tribal chiefs. Early Christian teachers had
to contend with 'a tissue of magical practices and rit-
uals, the observation of omens, the use of spells and
incantatory formulas and the avoidance of unlucky
actions'. (de Paor, p.29) It might have been expected
that missionary bishops like Patrick would have
received a hostile reception – Patrick wrote about
dangers and expected martyrdom – but, by and large,
the Irish were too taken up with internal political
struggles to think of eliminating Christian preachers.

Patrick tells very little about his work among the Christian community, much more about the conversions, baptisms and ordinations among the pagans, an aspect of ministry to which he seems to have devoted himself. This emphasis in his work may have been one of the reasons why he came under sharp criticism – British church leaders may have expected him to concentrate on building up the existing church. He was so single-minded in his service to the Irish that he resolved never to leave Ireland but to spend the rest of his life there.

His writings

Both the *Confession* and the *Letter to Coroticus* date from late in his life. Patrick was no theologian and, his education having been severely disrupted, his command of Latin, the universal language of the learned, was extremely shaky. He tells us himself that he hesitated to write, for fear of ridicule, but eventually felt obliged to write the *Confession* to proclaim God's goodness to him and to defend himself against his critics.

The Letter to Coroticus is a letter of excommunication against a British ruler, whose soldiers had abducted into slavery some of Patrick's newly-baptised converts. Written in haste and in anger, it affords little scope for devotional use.

The prayer-poem *St Patrick's Breastplate* is attributed traditionally to St Patrick, but scholars are agreed that it is in fact a later work.

Early writings about Patrick

The ninth-century manuscript, *The Book of Armagh*, now one of the treasures of the Library of Trinity College, Dublin, was known as 'Patrick's testament'. As well as the *Confession*, it includes Muirchu's *Life of Patrick* and Tirechan's *Memoirs and Sayings*. They are the source of much of the Patrician tradition and legend.

Patrick's achievements

Patrick claimed that, as a result of his mission to the west of Ireland, 'the gospel has been preached to those places beyond which nobody lives', (*Conf* 34, de Paor, p.102) believing that the whole earth had now been evangelised and that the end of the world was, therefore, imminent.

The reader may find it frustrating that we know so little about Patrick's ministry. The picture he gives may be incomplete, but it is the earliest firsthand picture of a Christian in Ireland, indeed of any person in Ireland. It is also the first picture of any *British* Christian.

For all his knowledge of Ireland, Patrick was a British Christian. It seems that his version of the Creed, taught and accepted among the Irish, was the Rule of Faith of the British church. Perhaps his greatest achievement was adapting Romano-British Christianity to the realities of Irish life, so that a new and distinctive Irish church emerged, which provided hope during the dark ages which enveloped Europe from the fifth century on.

Patrick's Spirituality

Patrick had a simple faith and a compulsion to share it. He trusted in God, Father, Son and Holy Spirit, to supply all his needs, he lived for God and would have been happy to die for God. He had a very thorough knowledge of the Bible and probably drew on it as constantly in his teaching as he did in his writing.

From the time of his captivity he based his life on prayer. It was through prayer that he discovered God's will and gained the strength to do it.

Patrick was a humble man, well aware of his own shortcomings, but he believed that grace is a transforming gift which enables the believer to do great things in God's service.

As our redemption cost Christ his life, Patrick believed that wholeheartedness was the only possible response. As Christ had warned, no-one can serve two masters – half measures are not good enough.

Author's Note

Because of the clumsiness of Patrick's Latin, it is extremely difficult to render his meaning in good English. In preparing this book, I have used three translations: *The Life and Writings of the historical Saint Patrick* by R. P. C. Hanson (New York: Seabury Press, 1983); *Patrick in his own words* by Joseph Duffy (Dublin: Veritas, 1985); *St Patrick's World: The Christian Culture of Ireland's Apostolic Age: Translations and Commentaries* by Liam de Paor (Dublin: Four Courts, 1993; paperback edition, 1996).

Unless otherwise stated, the translations used here are by Hanson. Where I have used pieces from a number of translations, both translators' names are given. In a couple of instances I have used my own translation.

There are numerous allusions to the Latin text. This is highly significant in the study of Patrick's writings because he wove so many biblical phrases into his text, and because the Bible he used was a Latin translation. Although the version he used – a mixture of biblical, ecclesiastical and vulgar Latin – differs considerably from that on which modern translations are based, it does make it easy to discern the extent of Patrick's biblical spirituality.

Apart from the biblical texts which appear in Patrick's writings, the *New Revised Standard Version* is used throughout this book.

1. God's transforming work in us

ATRICK begins the *Confession* with the words: 'I am Patrick, a sinner, most uncultivated and least of all the faithful and most despised in the eyes of many.' (*Conf* 1) In some ways this is redolent of St Paul: 'I am the least of the apostles, unfit to be called an apostle,' (1 Cor 15:9) While it was an accepted form for religious writers of the time to protest their inferiority, Patrick's repeated admissions of inadequacy are clearly genuine and he shows constant wonder at God's transforming grace. 'Who am I, Lord, and what is my calling, since you have worked in me with such divine power?' (*Conf* 34)

He is very conscious of having deserted God in his youth, despite being born into a Christian family. 'We had deserted God and we had not observed his commandments and we had not been obedient to our bishops who used to warn us about our salvation.' (*Conf* 1) If he blamed this desertion of God for his captivity, he was all the more amazed at God's mercy to him in answering his prayers and enabling him to escape.

Patrick escaped more than physical slavery. He escaped into a transformed life of faith, built up by his life of prayer 'out in the woods or on the mountain.' (*Conf* 16)

God's transformation of Patrick was so complete that he could endure insults, persecutions and imprisonment and count them merely as the springboard for his work in Ireland.

While St Paul upbraided himself for having persecuted the church, Patrick felt inadequate because he lacked education and the eloquence to proclaim the gospel. Once he accepted that God was working in him, however, Patrick, like Paul, (1 Cor 4:10) was quite happy to be a fool, as long as he was a fool for Christ's sake.

Patrick's Words

The Spirit elsewhere is a witness that even uncultivated ways have been created by the Most High – I am, then, first and foremost unlearned, an unlettered exile who cannot plan for the future. But this much I know for sure. Before I had to suffer, I was like a stone lying in the deep mud. Then he who is mighty came and in his mercy he not only pulled me out but lifted me up and placed me at the very top of the wall. I must, therefore, speak publicly in order to thank the Lord for such wonderful gifts.

Who was it who called me, fool that I am, from among those who are considered wise, expert in law, powerful in speech and general affairs? He passed over these for me, a mere outcast. He inspired me with fear, reverence and patience, to be the one who would if possible serve the people faithfully to whom the love of Christ brought me. The love of Christ indeed gave me to them to

> serve them humbly and sincerely for my entire
> lifetime if I am found worthy. (*Conf* 12-13, Duffy,
> p.16)

Patrick clearly understood that this transformation
was God's work, not his own, that he would have
remained 'like a stone in deep mud' had not God
pulled him out and lifted him up.

The image of Christ as the cornerstone, and Christian
believers as part of the building of the Lord's temple,
is well known. Less well known is Patrick's other
source:

> Save me, O God,
> for the waters have come up to my neck.
> I sink in deep mire
> where there is no foothold.
> With your faithful help rescue me
> from sinking in the mire. (Ps 69:1-2,13b-14a)

> I waited patiently for the Lord;
> he inclined to me and heard my cry.
> He drew me out ... out of the miry bog,
> and set my feet upon a rock,
> making my steps secure. (Ps 40:1-2)

In claiming a complete inner transformation, Patrick
again reveals the influence of Pauline theology on
him:

> If anyone is in Christ, there is a new creation:
> everything old has passed away; see, everything has
> become new! All this is from God, who reconciled
> us to himself through Christ. (2 Cor 5:17)

While Patrick pictured his transformation in terms of a stone placed in the wall by God, other writers have used different metaphors. Hildegard of Bingen saw herself as a feather on the breath of God, being carried along as and where God chose. Teresa of Avila used the imagery of the silkworm, the cocoon and the butterfly, to teach that God's transformation of us happens stage by stage.

When Peter was called before the Sanhedrin to account for the healing of a cripple, he boldly proclaimed:

✠ This man is standing before you in good health by the name of Jesus Christ of Nazareth, whom you crucified, whom God raised from the dead. This Jesus is 'the stone that was rejected by you, the builders; it has become the cornerstone.' There is salvation in no-one else. (Acts 4:10-12. Peter was applying to Christ the imagery from Psalm 118:22.)

Paul took up the theme in his letter to the Ephesians (2:19-21):

✠ You are no longer strangers and aliens, but you are citizens with the saints and also members of the household of God, built upon the foundation of the apostles and prophets, with Christ Jesus himself as the cornerstone. In him the whole structure is joined together and grows into a holy temple in the Lord.

2. God as a threesome

ATRICK'S 'Rule of Faith' comes very early (*Conf* 4) in the *Confession*, partly to prove his credentials, but also because of its pivotal importance in his life. It expresses God's three acts of love: the first in creation, the second in sending Jesus Christ to redeem the world, the third in giving us the Holy Spirit as the giver of light and life.

Written in Latin far more polished than his own, it is clear that this credal statement was not composed by Patrick. The opening phrases conclude with 'as our formula runs', which suggests that he was using the Rule of Faith of the British church. In many ways it is similar to the Rule of Faith given in a book on the Revelation of St John the Divine by Victorinus, a bishop in the Balkans at the beginning of the fourth century. The second half is little more than an amalgam of five New Testament passages: Phil 2:9-12, Acts 10:42, Rom 2:6, Titus 3:5-6, Rom 8:16-17.

Patrick continues: 'I must teach from the rule of faith of the Trinity', (*Conf* 14) which is, in part, his way of interpreting Christ's call to mission. Winning the Irish from paganism and superstition was, indeed, Patrick's life's work. The Trinity provided his sole armour for the fight against:

the demon snares of sin

the vice that gives temptation force ...

the hostile men that mar my course …
in every place and in all hours.
(*St Patrick's Breastplate*,
versified translation by Mrs C. F. Alexander).

Patrick's Words

There is no other God, nor was there ever in the past nor will there be in the future, except God the Father ingenerate, without beginning, from whom all beginning flows, who controls all things, as our formula runs: and his Son Jesus Christ whom we profess to have existed with the Father, begotten spiritually before the origin of the world in an inexpressible way by the Father before all beginning, and through him were made things both visible and invisible; he was made man; when death had been overcome he was received into Heaven by the Father, and he gave to him all power above every name of things heavenly and earthly and subterranean and that every tongue should confess to him that Jesus Christ is Lord and God; and we believe in him and await his advent which will happen soon, as judge of the living and the dead, and he will deal with everybody according to their deeds and he poured out upon us richly the Holy Spirit, the gift and pledge of immortality, who makes those who believe and obey to be sons of God and coheirs with Christ and we confess and adore him, one God in the Trinity of sacred name. (*Conf* 4)

Irish Christians at home and overseas symbolise Patrick's teaching on the Holy Trinity by the shamrock. On St Patrick's Day (17 March) the Irish wear the shamrock on their lapels, in remembrance of the saint. The fact that the tradition is relatively modern, and that some scholars believe that the word derives from the Irish word *seam* (pronounced 'sham') for rivet, as in the three rivets of a pre-Christian sword found off Donegal, need not detract from the image of the shamrock for reflection on the Trinity.

Think of:

> the Three who are over me
> the Three who are below me
> the Three who are in front of me
> the Three who are behind me

This is a prayer pattern typical of Celtic spirituality, in which there were countless prayers to the Holy Trinity, particularly for early morning and late night devotions and in blessings. At their simplest they run like this:

> The grace of God be with you,
> The grace of Christ be with you,
> The grace of the Spirit be with you
> And with your children,
> For an hour, for ever, for eternity.
> (Esther de Waal, *The Celtic Vision, prayers and blessings from the Outer Hebrides, selections from the Carmina Gadelica*, London, 1985, p.247)

The way in which Celtic artistry depicted the Trinity is beautifully explained by George Otto Simms:

The patterned ornaments of the *Book of Durrow*, a treasure from a golden age of faith in our country, seem to express the completeness and perfection of the triune God. If 'three in one' makes nonsense in straightforward language, the roundels and ribboned interlacing of the decorated pages of this gospel book convey the sense of mystery and holiness that confronts the believer in a thrice-personed God. We see a perfect circle containing within its compass three smaller contiguous circles, proportionately placed, eloquent of unity and yet of diversity through an artistry that is abstract, yet far from lifeless.

(Lesley Whiteside, ed, *Through the Year with George Otto Simms*, Dublin, 1993, p.46)

✠ When we cry 'Abba! Father!' it is that very Spirit bearing witness with our spirit that we are children of God, and if children, then heirs, heirs of God and joint heirs with Christ – if, in fact, we suffer with him so that we may be glorified with him. (Rom 8:15b-17)

3. Christy the true sun

ATRICK was more than willing to face martyrdom: 'I may lack burial itself or my corpse may be most squalidly torn limb from limb by dogs or wild beasts, or the birds of the air may devour it.' He faced the possibility with the utmost confidence because 'without a shadow of doubt we shall rise in the radiance of the sun, that is, in the glory of Christ Jesus our Redeemer'. (*Conf* 59)

He went on to warn against sun-worship, which may have been an element in Celtic paganism. It certainly was a feature of most other early religions, and just as the early Church adapted pagan festivals and turned them into Christian festivals, the image of the sun was also adapted into Christian imagery. Thus Christ was represented as the sun in early Christian art, as well as in hymns and prayers. There is, in Saint Peter's Basilica in Rome, a fourth-century mosaic depicting Christ as the sun god, with golden rays radiating from his halo.

Patrick's Words

The sun which we see rises every day for our benefit at his behest, but it will never reign nor will its radiance endure, but all who worship it will come to a bad end. But we believe in and adore the true Sun, Jesus Christ, who will never die, nor will anyone die who has done his will ... (*Conf* 60)

Calling Christ 'the Sun' can be read as another way of saying that he is 'the light of the world'. Patrick may have been drawing on Isaiah:

> The sun shall no longer be your light by day,
> nor for brightness shall the moon
> give light to you by night;
> but the Lord will be your everlasting light,
> and your God will be your glory.
> Your sun shall no more go down
> or your moon withdraw itself;
> for the Lord will be your everlasting light.
> (Is 60:19-20)

If Christ the Sun shines on us, we grow and flourish, we blossom like the lilies of the field, producing the fruit of the Spirit. (Gal 5:22)

> Christ, whose glory fills the skies,
> Christ, the true, the only light,
> Son of righteousness, arise;
> Triumph o'er the shades of night:
> Day-spring from on high, be near,
> Day-star, in my heart appear.
> (*Charles Wesley*)

✠ Jesus spoke to them, saying:
I am the light of the world. Whoever follows me will never walk in darkness but will have the light of life. (Jn 8:12)

✠ In the beginning was the Word, and the Word was with God, and the Word was God. He was in the beginning with God. All things came through him, and without him not one thing came into being. What has come into being in him was life, and the life was the light of all people. The light shines in the darkness and the darkness did not overcome it.

There was a man sent from God, whose name was John. He came as a witness to testify to the light, so that all might believe through him. He himself was not the light, but he came to testify to the light. The true light, which enlightens everyone, was coming into the world. (Jn 1:1-9)

4. The power of the Spirit

ATRICK, in common with many early Christian writers, experienced the Holy Spirit as a divine fire glowing within him, warming the outer reaches of his soul and sparking off inspired ideas. He talks of the Spirit 'prompting' him, and enabling him to preach and write, by providing not only the inspiration but the very words. Likewise, when words fail him in prayer, he finds that the Spirit prays for him. He is strengthened by the belief that, when he has exhausted his own resources, the Spirit takes over and kindles new initiatives in him.

Muirchu's *Life of Patrick,* in the *Book of Armagh,* gives a vivid account of Patrick's confrontation with King Loegaire (pronounced Lay-re) at Tara. A pagan festival was to be held at Tara, coinciding with Easter. The king issued a prohibition on all fires and lights other than those which he would provide. Patrick had decided to celebrate the greatest Christian festival by lighting the traditional Paschal fire on the Hill of Slane, across the plains of Meath from Tara. The fire glowed in the dark and could be seen clearly by Loegaire and his elders in Tara. The king was furious and pronounced a death sentence on the one who had violated his command but (like the court of Nebuchadnezzar in the book of Daniel) his elders replied: 'O King, live for ever. The fire which we see was lit tonight before one was lit in your house, the palace of Tara: This fire will never be extinguished, unless it is put out tonight.' They warned the king that Patrick was going round the country preaching and baptising, but did not understand that the fire which they predicted would last until the end of the world was the fire of the Spirit and not one of wood. Loegaire marched towards Slane, accompanied by warriors and wizards, intending to kill the one who had defied his orders. Patrick, however, came to meet his attackers in the power of the Spirit and was able to enter the court of Tara unharmed.

Patrick's Words

But when I had come by ill luck to Ireland ... every day I used to look after sheep and I used to pray often during the day, the love of God and the fear of him increased more and more [in me] and my faith began to grow ... so that in one day [I would say] as many as a hundred prayers and nearly as many at night ... and I used to rise before dawn for prayer, in snow and frost and rain, and I used to feel no ill effect and there was no slackness in me (as I now realise, it was because the Spirit was glowing in me). (*Conf* 16)

That night, when I was asleep, Satan tempted me most severely. It was as if a huge rock fell on top of me and I had no use of my limbs ... [but] I believe that the Lord Jesus came to my help, and that it was the Spirit who was already crying out in me; and I pray that it will be so on the day of my troubles, as it says in the gospel: 'It is not you who speaks but the Spirit of the Father who speaks within you.' (*Conf* 20, de Paor, p.100. Patrick is quoting Matthew 10:19-20)

I ought not to hide the gift of God, which he has lavished upon us in the land of our captivity, because I then sought him resolutely and there I found him, and he preserved me from all forms of wickedness because of his indwelling Spirit, who has been active in me up to this day. (*Conf* 33)

The imagery of divine fire comes from the account in Acts of the day of Pentecost, when the advent of the Holy Spirit was accompanied by 'tongues as of fire'. This imagery has captured the imagination of Christians, writers and artists through the centuries. Thus people have yearned to have fire in their hearts, or to glow with fire divine. This fire is a source of catharsis or purification and of energy.

Holy Spirit, love divine,
Glow within this soul of mine;
Kindle every high desire;
Perish self in thy pure fire.
(*Samuel Longfellow*)

The second and third excerpts from Patrick's writings above show that his understanding is very close to St John's concept of the Holy Spirit as *paracletos* (John 14:16, 26, 15:26, 16:7), variously translated as comforter (from the Latin *fortis*, so that the Spirit is the one who strengthens and emboldens rather than one who soothes), counsellor, helper, advocate, even as defence lawyer.

✠ When the day of Pentecost had come, they were all together in one place. And suddenly from heaven there came a sound like the rush of a violent wind, and it filled the entire house where they were sitting. Divided tongues, as of fire, appeared among them, and a tongue rested on each of them. All of them were filled with the Holy Spirit and began to speak in other languages, as the Spirit gave them ability. (Acts 2:1-4)

✠ The Spirit helps us in our weakness; for we do not know how to pray as we ought, but that very Spirit intercedes with sighs too deep for words. And God, who searches the heart, knows what is the mind of the Spirit, because the Spirit intercedes for the saints according to the will of God. (Rom 8:26-27)

5. God's fishers and hunters

ATRICK'S call to mission was quite dramatic. After his escape from slavery, Patrick returned to live with his parents, who entreated him not to leave them again. A few years later, however, he had a dream one night in which a man called Victoricus stood in front of him. In his hand he held a great sheaf of letters, one of which he gave to Patrick.

'I read the heading of the letter which ran, "The Cry of the Irish," and, while I was reading aloud the heading of the letter, I was imagining that at that very moment I heard the voice of those who were by the Wood of Voclut which is near the Western Sea, and this is what they cried, as with one voice, "Holy boy, we are asking you to come and walk among us again," and I was struck deeply to the heart and I was not able to read any further and at that I woke up. God be thanked that after several years the Lord granted to them according to their cry.' (*Conf* 23)

Patrick's Words
We must fish well and steadily, just as the Lord warns us and teaches us when he says: 'Follow me and I will make you fishers of men'; and in another place he says through the prophets: 'Look! I send fishers and many hunters', says God, and so on. That is why we are strictly bound to spread our nets, so that an abundant multitude should be

caught for God and that there should be clergy everywhere who should baptise and preach to the needy and expectant masses. As the Lord says in the gospel: 'Go therefore and teach all nations, baptising them in the name of the Father and of the Son and of the Holy Spirit, teaching them to observe all things, whatever I have taught you.' (*Conf* 40)

When Christ called Simon Peter and Andrew, James and John to be his first disciples, they were fishing on the Sea of Galilee. His call to come and fish for people struck a chord with them at once because he spoke to their condition. Likewise, Patrick's image of fishing and hunting (which he borrowed from Jeremiah 16:16) fitted in well with Irish society at the time, for everyone would have been familiar with the imagery.

'We must fish well and steadily,' he says, conjuring up the fishers casting the nets from their small boats again and again, patiently waiting for a good catch. Implied is the subsequent rejoicing when the catch is brought safely home.

The hunting reference has a slightly different emphasis: rather than waiting patiently, the hunter has to travel widely, perhaps over hill and mountain, across rivers and through woods, to make his catch.

In Carnalway (pronounced 'carn-all-way'), County Kildare, a stained glass window by Harry Clarke depicts, in one panel of sapphire glass, St Hubert kneeling in a moonlit forest before a stag. Between the stag's antlers there rises a stark cross. Legend runs that Hubert, patron-saint of huntsmen, was out hunting on Good Friday, when this encounter with the stag brought him to his knees and led to his conversion. He dismounted his horse and knelt in awe. The hunter was hunted ... by Christ. He saw the empty cross of the risen Christ in the animal he had been chasing.

In linking this fishing and hunting for people with Christ's great commission to the eleven disciples before his ascension ('Go therefore and teach all nations' Mt 28:19-20), Patrick was emphasising both the evangelistic and the formal elements of his calling, a calling not only to carry the gospel far and wide but also to set up a continuing church by baptising new members and by ordaining clergy.

✠ As Jesus passed along the Sea of Galilee, he saw Simon and his brother casting a net into the sea – for they were fishermen. And Jesus said to them, 'Follow me and I will make you fish for people.' And immediately they left their nets and followed him. (Mk 1:16-18)

Luke's version tells of Christ seeing two boats on the shore:

✠ He got into one of the boats, the one belonging to Simon, and asked him to put out a little way from the shore. Then he sat down and taught the crowds from the boat. When he had finished speaking, he said to Simon: 'Put out into the deep water and let down your nets for a catch.' Simon answered: 'Master, we have worked all night long but have caught nothing. Yet if you say so, I will let down the nets.' When they had done this, they caught so many fish that their nets were beginning to break. So they signalled their partners in the other boat to come and help them. And they came and filled both boats, so that they began to sink. But when Simon Peter saw it, he fell down at Jesus's knees, saying: 'Go away from me, Lord, for I am a sinful man!' For he and all who were with him were amazed at the catch ....

Then Jesus said to Simon: 'Do not be afraid, from now on you will be catching people.' When they had brought their boats to the shore, they left everything and followed him. (Lk 5:3-11)

6. Spend and be spent

NE OF the criticisms levelled against Patrick was that he had profited financially from his mission in Ireland. Stung to the core at any suggestion of misuse of funds, or, worse, of embezzlement, he devoted a considerable part of the *Confession* to refuting the charges.

He readily admits that Irish Christians often gave him 'voluntary gifts' and 'used to throw some of their jewellery on the altar,' but he asserts that they were annoyed that he insisted on giving it back and, further, that he 'took advantage of none of them'. (*Conf* 48-49)

He challenges his critics to prove that he expected 'as much as a ha'penny' from any of the thousands he baptised. (*Conf* 50, de Paor, p.106) On the contrary, in order to continue his mission, he often made payments for safe conduct, and in that way incurred considerable expense. Indeed he spent himself in travelling to far-flung areas to preach the gospel.

Patrick's Words

You have experience of how much I paid out to those who administered justice in all the districts that I used to visit often. I reckon that I spent among them not less than the price of fifteen men, in order that you should enjoy me and I

> should always enjoy you in God. I do not regret it
> and it is not enough. I am still spending and will
> spend to the limit. The Lord is powerful enough
> to grant me later to spend myself for your souls.
> (*Conf* 53)

The verb which Patrick uses, *impendo,* and the
stronger *superimpendo,* convey the idea of giving until
there is nothing left to give, of exhausting one's energy
and resources, of holding nothing back.

When Patrick professes himself ready to spend himself for the souls of others, he is close to Paul's idea of
spending and being spent. (2 Cor 12:15) In fact, the
whole defence of his financial rectitude is closely
modelled on Paul's defence of *his* ministry to the
Corinthians:

> Here I am, ready to come to you this third time.
> And I will not be a burden, because I do not want
> what is yours but you ... I will gladly spend and
> be spent for you ... Nevertheless (you say) since I
> was crafty, I took you in by deceit. Did I take
> advantage of any of you through any of those
> whom I sent you? ... Everything we do, beloved,
> is for the sake of building you up. (2 Cor 12:14-
> 17, 19b)

Apart from the military overtones, Ignatius Loyola's
prayer might almost have been written by Patrick:

> Teach us, good Lord,
> to serve you as you deserve,
> to give and not to count the cost,
> to fight and not to heed the wounds,

to toil and not to seek for rest,
to labour and not to ask for any reward,
save that of knowing that we do your will,
through Jesus Christ our Lord.

✠ [Jesus] told them a parable: 'The land of a rich man produced abundantly. And he thought to himself, "What shall I do, for I have no place to store my crops?" Then he said, "I will do this: I will pull down my barns and build larger ones, and there I will store all my grain and my goods, and I will say to my soul, 'Soul, you have ample goods laid up for many years; relax, eat, drink, be merry.'" But God said to him, "You fool! This very night your life is being demanded of you. And the things you have prepared, whose will they be?" So it is with those who store up treasures for themselves but are not rich towards God.' (Lk 12:16-21)

✠ Do not be afraid, little flock, for it is your Father's good pleasure to give you the kingdom. Sell your possessions and give alms. Make purses for yourselves that do not wear out, an unfailing treasure in heaven, where no thief comes near and no moth destroys. For where your treasure is, there your heart will be also. (Lk 12:32-34)

7. A slave of Christ

I N CALLING himself Christ's slave, Patrick was not indulging in pietism, for he knew what slavery was all about. Having been brought up in a well-to-do home, the shock of his abduction into slavery must have been shattering. His account is short and terse:

'My father had a small estate, where I was taken captive. I was then barely sixteen. I had neglected the true God, and when I was carried off into captivity in Ireland, along with a great number of people, it was well deserved.' (*Conf* 1, de Paor, p.96)

We know very little about those years of slavery, spent as a shepherd in a remote place. There is no suggestion that his master was particularly cruel – perhaps even, he was quite kind because Patrick says he 'deserted the man with whom I had been for six years,' (*Conf* 17) and this implies a sense of loyalty to his master. Cruel or kind, the worst aspect of his slavery, apart from his separation from home and loved ones, must have been the lack of freedom, being bound to do the will of another. The divine irony is that, having obtained his freedom, he subsequently returned to the land of his captivity, bound in the Spirit and a slave of a greater master, Jesus Christ.

Patrick's Words
It cannot be thought that I came to Ireland without God or on purely secular business! Who com-

pelled me? I was bound in the Spirit so as never to revisit any of my kinspeople.

I was a free man in worldly position; my father was a decurion. Indeed I bargained away my aristocratic status ... for the benefit of others. In short I am a slave in Christ. (*Letter*, 10)

Slaves were often chained at night to prevent them running away; sometimes they were even obliged to work in chains.

The chains with which Patrick was bound in the Spirit did not tie him to God against his will. They were rather love-ties which bound him to God, a spiritual umbilical cord.

As Patrick knew from experience, slaves were regarded as chattels. A master had complete control over his slave, from whom he expected absolute obedience, to the point of perfect submission. It was this obedience and submission which Patrick offered to God, in response to his love. Being a slave in Christ meant to Patrick freedom from himself. In self-denial he found the key to self-fulfilment.

As George Matheson wrote:

Make me a captive, Lord,
And then I shall be free.

The nature of that freedom is well explained by George Appleton:

Freedom in Christ is not freedom to do what I like but freedom to be what I am meant to be.
It is freedom from the chains

which have held me back
from being my true self.
(*Journey for a Soul,* Glasgow,1974, p.181)

The absolute obedience of Patrick prefigured that of the medieval monks. From Comgall's monastery at Bangor, through the Rule of Columbanus to the later Franciscans, the type of obedience expected was that of a slave, with the all-important proviso that it was a servitude willingly and lovingly offered.

Eternal God,
you are the light of the minds that know you,
the joy of the hearts that love you
and the strength of the wills that serve you;
grant us so to know you that we may truly love you,
and so to love you that we may fully serve you,
whom to serve is perfect freedom,
in Jesus Christ our Lord.
(Prayer after Saint Augustine)

✠ Jesus called [the disciples] to him and said, 'You know that the rulers of the Gentiles lord it over them, and their great ones are tyrants over them. It will not be so among you; but whoever wishes to be great among you must be your servant, and whoever wishes to be first among you must be your slave; just as the Son of Man came not to be served but to serve, and to give his life as a ransom for many.' (Mt 20:25-28)

✠ Let the same mind be in you that was in Christ Jesus, who, though he was in the form of God, did not regard equality with God as something to

be exploited, but emptied himself, taking the
form of a slave, being born in human likeness.
And being found in human form, he humbled
himself and became obedient to the point of
death – even death on a cross. (Phil 2:5-8)

8. God with us

HROUGHOUT his ministry, Patrick had a strong sense of God's presence with him and in him. In fact, he came to realise that God had been the inner presence who, even before Patrick came to faith, strengthened and comforted him 'as a father comforts his son'. (*Conf* 2)

'I have recognised him', (*Conf* 3) says Patrick, affirming that his relationship with God is a close, personal one. God has reformed, moulded, taught and guided him every step of the way and it is God whom he trusts for strength in every situation. He even talks of throwing himself into God's hands, just as a frightened child hurls himself into the safety of his father's arms. (*Conf* 55)

Patrick's experience of an indwelling God was coupled with the sense that God pervades the universe. In this respect, he shared the Celtic belief that God is everywhere, in all people and in all creation for ever.

So Patrick goes out in the strength of:
    The virtues of the starlit heaven,
    The glorious sun's life-giving ray,
    The whiteness of the moon at even,
    The flashing of the lightning free,
    The whirling wind's tempestuous shocks,
    The stable earth, the deep salt sea,
    Around the old eternal rocks.
    (*The Breastplate*, translated by C.F. Alexander)

Patrick's Words

While *St Patrick's Breastplate* is attributed to the saint and closely associated with him in tradition, scholars agree that it was not in fact written by Patrick. However, the following verse reflects his spirituality:

> Christ be with me,
> Christ within me,
> Christ behind me,
> Christ before me,
> Christ beside me,
> Christ to win me,
> Christ to comfort and restore me.

Many spiritual disciplines use mantras. 'Christ be with me' or 'Christ within me' are the Christian equivalent – phrases that bear repeating again and again until they sink into your mind and heart.

The Breastplate is in the spirit of the Celtic *caim* (encompassment), an imaginary circle drawn around you with the forefinger of the right hand, in the belief that the circle safeguarded you wherever you went. Thus Christ is behind ... before ... beside ... beneath ... above ... The repetitive pattern of the prayer was an ordered adaptation of pagan incantations.

This type of prayer was used in early Christian communities in Ireland and Scotland, because it was a counter to spells and incantations with which their neighbours sought to ward off evil. For Christians such as Patrick, life was also full of dangers but *they* relied on *God* to protect them. Since its early days, the Christian church had taken over pagan festivals and customs, adapted them and incorporated them into its own practices.

The following prayer by David Adam seeks a sense of God's encircling presence.

> Circle me O God
> Keep hope within
> Despair without.
>
> Circle me O God
> Keep peace within
> Keep turmoil out.
>
> Circle me O God
> Keep calm within
> Keep storms without.
>
> Circle me O God
> Keep strength within
> Keep weakness out.
> (*The Cry of the Deer*, London, 1987, pp.13-15)

✠ O Lord, you have searched me and known me.
You know when I sit down and when I rise up;
You discern my thoughts from far away.
You search out my path and my lying down,
and are acquainted with all my ways.
Even before a word is on my tongue,
O Lord, you know it completely.
You hem me in, behind and before,
and lay your hand upon me.
Such knowledge is too wonderful for me …
(Ps 139:1-6)

✠ I am standing at the door knocking: If you hear
my voice and open the door, I will come in to you
and eat with you, and you with me. (Rev 3:20)

9. On the way

ATRICK had the pilgrim's sense of always being on a journey, and he firmly believed that God led him every step of the way. His attitude is illustrated in his words of encouragement to the crew of the ship which had taken him from Ireland after his escape:

'After three days we reached land. We travelled for twenty-eight days through a wilderness. They ran out of food, and hunger weakened them, and the next day the captain addressed me. "What's this, Christian? You say your God is great and all-powerful. Then why can't you pray for us? For we are in danger of dying of hunger. In fact it's doubtful if we'll see another human being." I said to them confidently: "Trust in the Lord my God and turn to him with all your hearts – since nothing is impossible for him – that he may send you today more than sufficient food for your journey – for he has an abundance everywhere."' (*Conf* 19, de Paor, p.99)

Whether it was a physical journey, as in returning to Ireland on his mission, or the next step in his work, Patrick saw himself as a traveller led and accompanied by God. He talked of travelling 'everywhere' even to the most remote parts 'through many dangers', (*Conf* 51) so that he daily expected to be 'killed, betrayed or brought back into slavery'. (*Conf* 55, de Paor, p.107) He was not fearful, however, because of the knowledge that Christ was with him.

Patrick's Words

We continue the meditative prayer of *The Breastplate:*

> Christ be with me,
> Christ within me,
> Christ behind me,
> Christ before me,
> Christ beside me,
> Christ to win me,
> Christ to comfort and restore me.
>
> Christ beneath me,
> Christ above me,
> Christ in quiet,
> Christ in danger,
> Christ in hearts of all that love me,
> Christ in mouth of friend and stranger.

As Patrick found, Christ is our companion *and* the way on life's journey.

> With that source of encouragement:
> 'All of life is a journey, full of new encounters and new experiences. As we travel we discover more about ourselves and others and life itself.
> But life is not meant to be just aimless wandering. We have a destination!'
> (*Celebrating Together: Prayers, Liturgies and Songs from Corrymeela,* Belfast, 1987, p.23)
>
> Christ in hearts of all that love me,
> Christ in mouth of friend and stranger.

We are Christ for friend and stranger alike, in a way which is best expressed by Teresa of Avila:

> Christ has no body on earth but yours,
> No hands but yours, no feet but yours.
> Yours are the eyes through which is to look out
> Christ's compassion for the world.
> Yours are the feet with which he is to go about
>   doing good.
> Yours are the hands with which he is to bless us
>   now.

✠ [Jesus said to the disciples]: 'In my Father's house there are many dwelling places. If it were not so, would I have told you that I go to prepare a place for you? And if I go and prepare a place for you, I will come again and will take you to myself, so that where I am, there you may be also. And you know the way to the place where I am going'. But Thomas said to him, 'Lord, we do not know where you are going. How can we know the way?' Jesus said to him, 'I am the way, the truth and the life. No one comes to the Father except through me.' (Jn 14:2-6)

10. A letter of Christ

ALTHOUGH Patrick was acutely aware of his academic deficiencies, his acceptance of the call to mission and the criticism he encountered eventually compelled him to write. The *Confession* was both a justification of his life's work and a celebration of God's goodness. 'I cannot remain silent,' he says, 'about the great favours and graces which the Lord deigned to grant me in the land of my captivity. For the way to make repayment for that revelation of God, through capture and enslavement, is to declare and make known his wonders to every race under heaven.' (*Conf* 3, de Paor, p.96)

Steeped in the scriptures as he was, Patrick realised the importance of the written word in carrying on the faith. The Bible was a veritable treasure house to him and he drew heavily on the great letter writer, St Paul, from whom he borrowed the phrase 'a letter of Christ'. As he wrestled with words in his struggle to express himself, Patrick must have found strength in the belief that a Christian life is a letter for Christ, clearer and more compelling than the written word.

Patrick's Words

I have long had it in mind to write, but up to now I have hesitated; I was afraid lest I should fall under the judgement of mens' tongues, because I am not well read as others are ... For our speech has been translated into a foreign tongue, as can easily be demonstrated from the savour of my writing, the extent of my education and learning. (*Conf* 9)

For my sins prevented me from continuing to build on my early education. As a youth, indeed not much more than a beardless boy, I was taken captive; before I knew what to aim at, what to avoid. So, because of this, today I am ashamed, and agitated with fear, at exposing my lack of education; because I lack the fluency to express myself concisely, as my spirit longs to do and as I try with my heart and soul.

But, even if I had been given what was given to others, nevertheless, out of gratitude, I would not be silent. And if perhaps I seem to many people to be pushing myself forward, with my lack of knowledge and my lame language, yet it is indeed written: 'The stammering tongues will quickly learn to speak peace.'

How much more ought we not to aim at that, since, as it is written, we ourselves are 'the letter of salvation, even to the end of the earth' and, even if the language does not flow but is blocked and turgid, 'it is written on your hearts not with ink but with the Spirit of the living God.' (*Conf* 10-11, de Paor, pp.97-98)

It is interesting that Patrick chose to justify his poor command of language with the phrase, 'the stammering tongues will quickly learn to speak peace,' or, as it reads in the *New Revised Standard Version*, 'the tongues of stammerers will speak readily and distinctly.' It comes from a passage in Isaiah 32 which describes the future Messianic kingdom in which both physical and mental disabilities will be healed. Thus 'the minds of the rash will have good judgment' but fools will be recognised as such, 'for fools speak folly ... utter error concerning the Lord ... [and] leave the craving of the hungry unsatisfied'. Patrick may have been trying to express a belief that, while his imperfections in this life would have to await perfection in the next life, he could, nevertheless, teach the gospel and satisfy those who hungered for truth.

While there is a great body of Christian literature, ranging from Paul, through Patrick and Augustine, to Bonhoeffer and Barth, the gospels are, more than any other writings, the letters of Christ.

Until the spread of literacy, the people listened to God's word being read to them, for they couldn't read it themselves. Among the best visual aids were the stone high crosses found in Ireland, and, in other countries, stained glass windows. The most intricate visual aids, enjoyed by a privileged few, were the illuminated gospel books, of which the most famous is the *Book of Kells*. All the artists and scribes knew that this was God's work – a letter of Christ.

In the Book of Kells there is no picture of the resurrection but only the word 'Una', in the centre of the page, to denote the first day of the week, the day of resurrection. George Otto Simms describes the resurrection page of that book as follows (*Exploring the Book of Kells*, Dublin: 1988, pp.53-54).

Angels are guarding the capital letter U, one at each of its four corners. It looks at first like a dark, dull page, but out of the dim gloom the feet, the hands and the faces of the four angels, painted with white lead, shine out gleaming and bright. These angels are looking up and out from the page … They are alive and alert, not asleep, nor downcast. Their message is 'Christ is risen, he is not here. Why look for the living among the dead?' We also observe, in the top right-hand corner, that the fierce monster is speeding away out of the picture. The power of this enemy has been

overcome. The beast is on his way out, defeated
… The capital U, with a tangle of graceful birds
in the heart of the letter, and surrounded by
guardian angels, helps us to have a picture in our
minds of the empty tomb on the first Easter Day.

✠ Surely we do not need, as some do, letters of rec-
ommendation to you or from you, do we? You
yourselves are our letter, written on our hearts, to
be known and read by all; and you show that you
are a letter of Christ, prepared by us, written not
with ink but with the Spirit of the living God, not
on tablets of stone but on tablets of human hearts.
(2 Cor 3:1-3)

11. Coping with loss

ATRICK suffered a great deal of loss in his life. As a youth, when carried off into slavery in Ireland, he lost family, friends, home and security. After years of slavery he was reunited with his family, who 'asked me whether – after such tribulations as I had undergone – they could trust me now as a son never to leave them again'. (*Conf* 23, de Paor, p.100) Before long, however, Patrick received God's call to return to Ireland and left his family and home for ever. Unlike the first occasion, when he had no choice, this time he had the difficult task of breaking the news, explaining his reasons and saying goodbye. There must have been an acute sense of loss on both sides.

Although he continued to miss his family, Patrick was stern with himself and was strengthened by the conviction that he was engaged in God's work. Yet the searing pain of loss is evident in a major incident later in his life.

A friend from childhood betrayed an adolescent confidence and disgraced Patrick before his fellow bishops. 'They found a pretext from thirty years earlier, bringing against me a confession I made before I was a deacon. Because, in an anxious and melancholy state of mind, I had privately told my dearest friend about something I had done one day – indeed in one hour – when I was a boy, before I had strength of character.' (*Conf* 27, de Paor, p.101)

Patrick's Words

I tell you boldly that my conscience does not reproach me ... but I am all the more sorry for my close friend: How did we deserve to hear such evidence given? He to whom I entrusted my very soul! And before that case, I learned from some of my brethren that it was he who would act on my behalf in my absence. (He is the very one who told me, with his own mouth: 'Look: you should be raised to the rank of bishop,' of which I was not worthy.) But how did he come, shortly afterwards, in public, in the presence of people both good and bad, to bring me into disgrace over something which he had willingly and gladly forgiven – as had the Lord, who is greater than all? (*Conf* 32, de Paor, p.102)

Patrick seems to have accepted that losses are an inevitable part of life and that they had to some extent moulded his character. Like Paul, he was able to set them aside for the greater joy of God's service. The loss of his dearest friend was probably the most severe test of Patrick's faith. Anger, bitterness, fear, loneliness follow such a betrayal of love and tend to make one determined not to suffer like that again. There certainly is a streak of loneliness and vulnerability in Patrick's writings.

Jesus made himself extremely vulnerable during his earthly life. He kept loving, giving himself, despite the fact that he knew that none of his disciples would stand by him in crisis. He suffered enormous loss in the Garden of Gethsemane when Peter, James and John proved unable to watch with him and slept through his agony, in Judas's kiss of betrayal, in Peter's denial and in the whole process which culminated in his crucifixion and final cry of desolation at Calvary.

Yet Jesus was able to view his loss in the context of God's overall plan:

> The tree of shame was made the tree of glory;
> and where life was lost, there life has been restored.
> *(The Alternative Service Book, 1980)*

✠ And when they had crucified him, they divided his clothes among themselves by casting lots; then they sat down there and kept watch over him .... Those who passed by derided him, shaking their heads and saying, 'You who would destroy the temple and build it in three days, save yourself! If you are the Son of God, come down from the cross.' In the same way the chief priests also, along with the scribes and elders, were mocking him, saying, 'He saved others; he cannot save himself. He is the King of Israel; let him come down from the cross now, and we will believe in him. He trusts in God; let God deliver him now, if he wants to; for he said "I am God's Son."' The bandits who were crucified with him also taunted him in the same way.

From noon on, darkness came over the whole

land until three o'clock in the afternoon. And about three o'clock Jesus cried with a loud voice, 'Eli, Eli, lema sabachthani?' that is, 'My God, my God, why have you forsaken me?'
(Mt 27:35-36, 39-46)

✠ I regard everything as loss because of the surpassing value of knowing Christ Jesus my Lord. For his sake I have suffered the loss of all things, and I regard them as rubbish, in order that I may gain Christ. (Phil 3:8-9)

12. The apple of God's eye

ATRICK was devastated when his friend's betrayal led to rejection by his seniors and, that very night, he had a dream in which he saw a coin with his own face on it and an inscription round the edge. In the days of the Roman Empire coins bore the face of the Emperor and an eulogistic inscription in his honour. At first, all Patrick could see was an accusatory inscription on the coin but then he heard God's voice assuring him that he was the apple of God's eye. In the midst of humiliation and disgrace God showed his approval.

Patrick's Words

That night I saw in a vision of the night a dishonouring inscription placed against my face, and at the same time I heard God's voice saying to me: 'We have seen with disapproval the face of the chosen one deprived of his good name.' He did not say 'you have disapproved' but 'we have disapproved', as if to include himself. As he says: 'He who touches you touches the apple of my eye.' (*Conf* 29 Hanson, Duffy, pp.24-25)

Patrick draws the phrase, 'the apple of my eye', from Zechariah (2:8), who had a similar confirmation of God's approval in a time of trial. In classical mythology the much-sought-after prize for the most beautiful woman was a golden apple. In Proverbs (25:11) 'a word fitly spoken is like apples of gold in a setting of silver'.

Likewise, apples feature in the erotic love poetry used in the Song of Solomon to convey to us the intensity of God's love for us:

> Oh, may your breasts be like clusters of the vine,
> and the scent of your breath like apples,
> and your kisses like the best wine
> that goes down smoothly,
> gliding over lips and teeth. (7:8-9)

This is the language of desire, much more familiar to us in poetry and the novel than in the Bible, but it tells us that God desires us passionately as individuals. The amazing thing is that God desires *each* of us with that intensity.

Some Christians find the Song of Solomon uncomfortable and prefer the more conventional terminology of God choosing us, along the lines of Isaiah 41:9: 'You are my servant, I have chosen you.' Yet Isaiah goes on to assure the chosen servant of God's help and protection in words which are very like human endearments: 'Here is my servant, whom I uphold, my chosen, in whom my soul delights' (Is 42:1); 'I have taken you by the hand and kept you' (Is 42:6); 'Do not fear, for I have redeemed you; I have called you by name, you are mine.' (Is 43:1)

Patrick often referred to himself as chosen by God. Usually he emphasised his unworthiness – 'he has even chosen me for this post that I should be among his lowest servants,' (*Conf* 56) but, on occasion, it was vital for him to know that God delighted in him, as the apple of his eye. The way in which the eighteenth-century former slave-trader, John Newton, celebrated the fact that God delighted in *him*, despite his short-comings, is reminiscent of Saint Patrick:

> Amazing grace! How sweet the name
> That saved a wretch like me.
> I once was lost, but now am found,
> Was blind, but now I see.

> ✠ [The Lord] sustained him in a desert land,
>   in a howling wilderness waste;
>   he shielded him, cared for him,
>   guarded him as the apple of his eye.
>   As an eagle stirs up its nest,
>   and hovers over its young;
>   as it spreads it wings, takes them up,
>   and bears them aloft on its pinions,
>   the Lord alone guided him. (Deut 32:10-12)

> ✠ I call upon you, for you will answer me, O God ...
>   Wondrously show your steadfast love ...
>   Guard me as the apple of the eye;
>   hide me in the shadows of your wings.
>   (Ps 17:6-8)

13. Perseverance

PATRICK did not find the Christian life easy. Often subject to temptation, he wrote; 'I do not trust myself as long as I am in this body of death, because he is so strong who daily strives to seduce me from my faith and the purity of a sincere religion which I have accepted from Christ my Lord to the end of my life. But the hostile flesh always draws me towards death, that is, towards enticements unlawful to indulge in. But ... up to this day, by the favour of the Lord, I have kept the faith.' (*Conf* 44)

He persevered through loneliness, criticism and discouragement, through danger and disaster. He clearly taught his converts to do the same and records with satisfaction that even those who were in slavery 'held out steadfastly against intimidation and threats.' (*Conf* 42)

His matter-of-fact accounts of his own brushes with death show his determination. Of one such episode he wrote:

'I used to give presents to kings in addition to what I used to give as a salary to their sons who used to travel around with me, and in spite of that they arrested me with my companions and on that occasion they were very anxious to kill me, but my time had not yet come, and they stole whatever they found in our possession, and they put me in irons and on the fourteenth day the Lord freed me from their power'. (*Conf* 52)

Patrick's Words

Let God never permit me to lose the people that he has won in the ends of the earth. I pray God to give me perseverance and to deign to allow me to give faithful testimony of him until my death. (*Conf* 58, de Paor, p.107)

I came to preach the gospel to Irish tribes and had to endure insults from unbelievers. I heard my mission scorned and suffered many persecutions, even to the point of being bound by chains, and gave up my status as a free man for the good of others. (*Conf* 37, my translation)

In the New Testament, perseverance is a major component of 'endurance', from the Latin *durare*, in which the emphasis is on holding out through hard times. Perseverance is also the attribute which enabled the members of the young church 'to continue steadfastly', as older translations ran and which is very much the language of Patrick.

Whether consciously or unconsciously, Patrick had Paul's example before him as he wrote these passages. 2 Timothy 2:8-11 reads:

That is my gospel, for which I suffer hardship, even to the point of being chained like a criminal. But the word of God is not chained. Therefore I endure everything for the sake of the elect, so that they may also obtain the salvation that is in Christ

Jesus with eternal glory. The saying is sure: If we
have died with him, we will also live with him.

In praying for perseverance, Patrick would also have
been familiar with the countless Old Testament
instances of human perseverance, from Abraham to
Daniel, and of God's perseverance, in infinite patience,
with humankind. He probably knew by heart passages from Isaiah (40:28-31), Micah (7:18-19), or
Hosea (14:4-7) which showed that, again and again,
in the face of indifference, God forgave, healed and
loved his people. From this store of divine precedent
he must have derived strength to persevere in dis-
couraging circumstances.

Jesus used the parable of the sower to illustrate the
importance of perseverance in our spiritual life. We
may not be the seed that falls on the path and per-
ishes, but most of us recognise ourselves, in part at
least, as that which falls on rocky ground or among
the thorns: We may have started enthusiastically to
serve God but have been discouraged by difficulties
or distracted by everyday responsibilities and by our
search for self-fulfilment. It is so easy to give up.

Among the enemies of perseverance are impatience
and boredom. This problem was addressed by the
seventeenth-century monk, Brother Lawrence, in
The Practice of the Presence of God. He was content
year after year to do the menial and repetitive jobs in
the kitchen, such as washing the pots and pans,
despite the fact that 'he had naturally a great aversion'
to the work, because he had learned 'to do everything
there for the love of God'. He continues:

We ought not to be weary of doing little things
for the love of God, for he regards not the great-
ness of the work, but the love with which it is per-
formed.

... That all things are possible to him who believes,
that they are less difficult to him who hopes, that
they are easier to him who loves, and still more
easy to him who perseveres in the practice of these
three virtues.

(Second conversation, 28 August 1666, fourth
conversation, 25 November 1667. My edition is
H. R. Allenson, London, n.d., but there are many
editions.)

✠ The sower sows the word. These are the ones on
the path where the word is sown: when they hear,
Satan immediately comes and takes away the
word that is sown in them. And these are the ones
sown on rocky ground: when they hear the word,
they immediately receive it with joy. But they
have no root and endure only for a while; then,
when trouble or persecution arises on account of
the word, immediately they fall away. And others
are those who are sown among the thorns: these
are the ones who hear the word, but the cares of
the world, and the lure of wealth, and the desire
for other things come in and choke the word, and
it yields nothing. And these are the ones sown on
the good soil: they hear the word and accept it
and bear fruit, thirty and sixty and a hundred-
fold. (Mk 4:14-20)

14. Thank God at all times

ATRICK concludes the *Confession* by asking that 'nobody shall ever say that it was I, the ignoramus, if I ever achieved ... any small success ... but that it was the gift of God.' (*Conf* 62) So great is Patrick's sense that it is in God's strength alone that he has been able to do anything worthwhile in life, that the *Confession* reads like a hymn of thanksgiving. He is thankful not for an easy life, a brilliant brain, protection from suffering and danger, but for God's loving presence and protection through all the weaknesses and difficulties with which he had to contend.

On the other hand, he is thankful that 'in Ireland a people who in their ignorance of God always worshipped idols and unclean things ... have now become a people of the Lord and are called children of God.' (*Conf* 41, Duffy, p.30))

One incident which gave him enormous pleasure was the coming to faith of an aristocratic woman, 'mature and beautiful, whom I baptised. A few days later ... she told us privately that she had received a message from an angel of God who commanded her to become a virgin of Christ and so draw nearer to him. Thanks be to God, just six days after that she embraced in the most excellent and eager way that which all the virgins of God follow.' (*Conf* 42, de Paor, p.104)

Patrick's Words

Who am I, Lord, or what am I called to, that in all your divinity you have shown yourself to me, so that today I constantly lift up and magnify your name among the heathen, wherever I have been, not only in good times but in bad? Whatever may happen to me, whether good or bad, I am equally bound to accept it and always give thanks to God because he has shown that I should believe in him endlessly as trustworthy. (*Conf* 34, de Paor, p.102, Hanson)

This, one of Patrick's most eloquent passages, is full of the same joy and thanksgiving as pervades Paul's letter to the Philippians. The message is the same:

We should exalt and glorify God's name …
wherever we happen to be …
not only when things go well but also in troubles …
giving thanks because God is trustworthy.

Thanksgiving at all times is much easier in theory than in practice. While Patrick positively welcomed troubles if they offered the prospect of martyrdom ('I greatly desire, indeed I long for, and am ready for him to grant me to drink this cup,' *Conf* 57, my translation), we are not expected to give thanks for the troubles, but thanks that God is with us through the troubles, even to the end.

In the glorious *Benedicite*, sung by Shadrach, Meshach and Abednego in the fiery furnace, God's deliverance was not *from* the furnace but *in* it. (Dan 3) God did not prevent them from being thrown into the flames, but was in the fire with them.

Edward Reynolds's *General Thanksgiving* captures exactly Patrick's spirit of thankfulness:

> Almighty God, Father of all mercies,
> we your unworthy servants
> give you most humble and hearty thanks
> for all your goodness and loving kindness.
> We bless you for our creation, preservation
> and all the blessings of this life;
> but above all, for your immeasurable love
> in the redemption of the world
> by our Lord Jesus Christ,
> for the means of grace, and for the hope of glory.
> And, give us, we pray,
> such a sense of all your mercies,
> that our hearts may be unfeignedly thankful,
> and that we show forth your praise,
> not only with our lips, but in our lives,
> by giving up ourselves to your service,
> and by walking before you
> in holiness and righteousness all our days;
> through Jesus Christ our Lord,
> to whom with you and the Holy Spirit,
> be all honour and glory, for ever and ever. Amen.
> (Bishop Edward Reynolds, *General Thanksgiving*,
> in *Alternative Service Book* version, amended)

✠ Enter his gates with thanksgiving
And his courts with praise;
Give thanks to him, bless his name.
For the Lord is good;
his steadfast love endures for ever,
and his faithfulness to all generations. (Ps 100:4-5)

✠ Be filled with the Spirit, as you sing psalms and hymns and spiritual songs among yourselves, singing and making melody to the Lord in your hearts, giving thanks to God the Father at all times and for everything in the name of the Lord Jesus Christ. (Eph 5:18-20)

15. The peace of the Lord

PEACE is scarcely mentioned in Patrick's writings, but his attitude to life is the same as St Paul's, who wrote, 'since we are justified by faith, we have peace with God through our Lord Jesus Christ.' (Rom 5:1) 'To set the mind on the Spirit is life and peace,' but, conversely, 'to set the mind on the flesh is death'. (Rom 8:6)

Patrick was so appalled at the actions of Coroticus and his soldiers, in carrying off Christian converts, that he could not bring himself to conclude his letter with the conventional blessing, so he finished: 'Peace to the Father and to the Son and to the Holy Spirit.' (*Letter* 21) In his awkward way, Patrick was grappling with the problems of sin. It was his sure conviction that he who commits vile deeds can find no peace, yet, while threatening Coroticus's soldiers with damnation, he held out the possibility of repentance and forgiveness – hence his half-enunciated invocation of peace.

Patrick's Words

Towards the end of the *Confession* there is a great sense of peace in Patrick's writing:

> I expect daily to be killed, betrayed, or brought back into slavery, or something of the kind. But, because of the promise of heaven, I fear none of

these things. For I have thrown myself into the hands of Almighty God, who reigns everywhere. As the prophet says, 'Cast your cares upon the Lord and he will sustain you.' (Ps 55:22) So now I commend my soul to my most trustworthy God, on whose behalf I am carrying out a mission. (*Conf* 55-56, de Paor, p.107, Hanson)

Patrick's words mirror those of Isaiah 26:3-4:

> Those of steadfast mind you keep in peace —
> in peace because they trust in you.
> Trust in the Lord forever,
> for in the Lord God
> you have an everlasting rock.

Better known in the older translation of anthems — 'Thou wilt keep him in perfect peace whose mind is stayed on thee' — the passage reflects Patrick's conviction that peace does not consist of rest and quiet, nor of the absence of war, but it is something for which we have to work.

Ostensibly there was very little peace in Patrick's life; he seems constantly to have been travelling from place to place, often in areas of inter-tribal strife, to have faced opposition to his ministry, threats from pirates and chiefs, a self-styled exile and refugee for the love of God and the Irish people.

Just as the peace which Christ gave him had been won at great cost, Patrick had discovered that he found peace through service and self-giving.

Christians through the centuries have found that Christ's peace is never easy:

> Lord, make us instruments of your peace:
> Where there is hatred, let us sow love;
> Where there is injury, pardon;
> Where there is doubt, faith;
> Where there is despair, hope;
> Where there is darkness, light;
> Where there is sadness, joy.
> (*Prayer of Saint Francis*)

Cecil and Myrtle Kerr, of the Christian Renewal Centre in Rostrevor, have for many years been involved in multi-denominational groups working for reconciliation in Ireland. Ponder a word of prophecy which Myrtle received at one such gathering:

> This is not an easy peace I would give you,
> my children.
> It cost me the cross to reconcile you to my Father.
> You must humble yourselves before each other,
> listen to each other's pain,
> share your brother's burden,
> seek his forgiveness,
> if you would really be reconciled in my love
> and my way.
> (Cecil Kerr, *The Way of Peace*, London, 1990,
> p.203)

Shortly before his passion, Jesus said to his disciples:

> ✠ Peace I leave with you; my peace I give to you.
> I do not give to you as the world gives.

Do not let your hearts be troubled,
and do not let them be afraid. (Jn 14:27)

✠ The hour is coming, indeed it has come, when
you will be scattered, each one to his home, and
you will leave me alone. Yet I am not alone
because the Father is with me. I have said this to
you, so that in me you may have peace. In the
world you face persecution. But take courage; I
have conquered the world! (Jn 16:32-33)

Acknowledgements

The author and publisher gratefully acknowledge the permission of the following to use copyright material: The Seabury Press for quotations from *The Life and Writings of the historical Saint Patrick* by R. P. C. Hanson; The Four Courts Press for quotations from *St Patrick's World* by Liam de Paor; Veritas Publications for quotations from *Patrick in his own words* by Joseph Duffy; Division of Christian Education, National Council of Churches of Christ in the United States of America for quotations from the *New Revised Standard Version* of the Bible; Darton, Longman and Todd for a quotation from *The Celtic Vision* by Esther de Waal; Harper-Collins Publishers for a quotation from *Journey for a Soul* by George Appleton; Triangle/ SPCK for a quotation from *Cry of the Deer* by David Adam; The Corrymeela Community for a quotation from *Celebrating Together;* The O'Brien Press for a quotation from *Exploring the Book of Kells* by George Otto Simms; Central Board of Finance of the Church of England for quotations from *The Alternative Service Book 1980;* Rev Cecil Kerr for a quotation from his *The Way of Peace.*